SOCIAL MEDIA MARKETING

How to use Social Media Marketing to Convert People into Customers

© Copyright 2018 by Carmine Rea - All rights reserved.

The following eBook is reproduced below with the goal of providing information that is as accurate and reliable as possible. Regardless, purchasing this e-book can be seen as consent to the fact that both the publisher and the author of this book are in no way experts on the topics discussed within and that any recommendations or suggestions that are made herein are for entertainment purposes only. Professionals should be consulted as needed prior to undertaking any of the action endorsed herein.

This declaration is deemed fair and valid by both the American Bar Association and the Committee of Publishers Association and is legally binding throughout the United States.

Furthermore, the transmission, duplication, or reproduction of any of the following work including specific information will be considered an illegal act irrespective of if it is done electronically or in print. This extends to creating a secondary or tertiary copy of the work or a recorded copy and is only allowed with an express written consent from the Publisher. All additional rights reserved.

The information in the following pages is broadly considered a truthful and accurate account of facts. As such, any inattention, use, or misuse of the information in question by the reader will render any resulting actions solely under their purview. There are no scenarios in which the publisher or the original author of this work can be in any fashion deemed liable for any hardship or damages that may befall them after undertaking information described herein.

Additionally, the information in the following pages is intended only for informational purposes and should thus be thought of as universal. As befitting its nature, it is presented without assurance regarding its prolonged validity or interim quality. Trademarks that are mentioned are done without written consent and can in no way be considered an endorsement from the trademark holder.

TABLE OF CONTENTS

Introduction 1

CHAPTER 1: Getting Started 3
What is Social Media Marketing? 3
How to Develop Your Goals with Social Media 4
The Best Tips to Improve Your Social Media Game 4

CHAPTER 2: It All Starts with a Plan 6
STEP 1: Identify the Correct Goals 7
STEP 2: Market Analysis and Competition Analysis 7
STEP 3: Voice and Style 8
STEP 4: The Tools and the Channel 8
STEP 5: Content Plan 8
STEP 6: Constant Check 9

CHAPTER 3: Being Consistent and Nine Other Important Aspects 11

CHAPTER 4: The Big Three – Instagram, Facebook, and YouTube 13
Instagram 13
    How to Succeed on Instagram 14
    Using a Business Account 14
    Instagram Biography: How to Write It 15

- The Importance of Storytelling 16
- Create a Content Marketing Strategy on Instagram 17
- Create an Editorial Plan and an Editorial Calendar...................... 18
- Interact with Followers and Create a Community 19
- How to Use Influencers 19
- Create Contest on Instagram... 20
- Stimulating Competition 20
- Interesting Prizes 20
- Studying a Promotion Strategy 20
- Instagram Stories: How to Exploit Them 21
- How to Measure the Results 22

Facebook 22

YouTube 25
- Create Interesting Videos 28
- Advertise the Channel 29
- Some Recommendations 30

Conclusion 32

INTRODUCTION

Congratulations on purchasing *Social Media Marketing: How to Use Social Media Marketing to Convert People into Customers*. Thank you for doing so.

The world of social media marketing is growing increasingly chaotic. Downloading this book is the first step that you can take towards doing something about improving your writing. The first step will not always be the easiest, which is why the information you will find in the following chapters is so important to take to heart, as they are not concepts that can be put into action immediately. If you file these concepts away for when you need them, you will be glad you have them at hand when the time comes to actually use them.

The following chapters will discuss the primary preparedness principles that you will need to consider if you ever hope to improve your social media marketing skills and unlock the power of social media. This means that you will want to consider the quality of your content, including the potential issues raised by the number of posts per day you make, how it can best be utilized to let your audience know about a product, as well as various strategies you might need to keep your audience engaged with the content they are consuming.

With quality out of the way, you will then learn everything you need to know about different tricks to improve your social media marketing skills.

I am happy to welcome you to the world of social media marketing and to help you unlock the hidden secrets of social networks.

CHAPTER 1:
GETTING STARTED

People today are used to get in touch with brands using social media. This means that having a powerful presence on those platforms and being able to tell the story of your brand adequately is the key to creating empathy and loyalty. If implemented correctly, social media marketing can help your company achieve your growth and reputation goals.

What is Social Media Marketing?

Social media marketing, or SMM, is a type of online marketing that uses a series of social networks to obtain a profitable and empathetic online advertising communication with users. Social media marketing retains users and customers by sharing textual content, images, and viral videos.

This book was created to provide useful information on social media marketing aimed at improving its business, giving businesses, businesses and accommodation businesses an operational tool with great advertising potentials at reduced costs.

Let's start with a plan!

Before starting to create a social media marketing campaign on Facebook, Instagram, YouTube, etc., you need to consider your sales and what you want to achieve. If you do not have a plan, you can be sure that you will get lost.

Here are some questions that you need to answer by yourself if you want to get ahead in the social media game:

- What are your goals?
- What do you know about your target audience?
- Where can you contact this target audience?
- What do you post on social media?
- What is the message you are trying to promote?

How to Develop Your Goals with Social Media

Social media marketing is a great tool to reach different goals. Here is a list of the most common ones:

- Increased traffic profiled towards your company website
- Increase in leads and conversions
- Increase of the recognition of your brand
- Building the proper reputation for your project
- Communicate and interact empathically with your customers

The Best Tips to Improve Your Social Media Game

Here you can find a list of some social media marketing tips that will help you to get your bearings right during all your campaigns.

Planning
As we mentioned previously, it is crucial to start building a social media marketing plan from the start. It is necessary to identify the keywords, ideas, and contents that could be of interest to the target audience.

Content
Content is the most important factor. If you want to be a successful online marketer, then you cannot underestimate the importance of high-quality content. Be sure to provide

interesting and vital information to your customers. Create different types of content using images, videos, and infographics, as well as classic content marketing.

Consistency
Using social media for marketing allows your company to advertise brands and products across a wide range of channels. Even if each platform has its own rules and environment, the core of your online communication must remain similar for all channels.

Blog
A blog or a website is a fundamental piece of every social media marketing strategy. The beauty of having a blog is that you own the space and you can publish everything you want in it.

Link
Although the use of social media for marketing is mainly based on the unique and original sharing of content concerning its business, to gain more followers and fans, it is also excellent for linking external articles. If other websites or companies offer information that you think is valuable to your audience, it is useful to create a dedicated link. The connection to external sources improves trust and reliability, and it is also possible to receive the same favor.

Keeping Track of the Competition
Monitoring what other similar brands are doing is the first step to be a step ahead of your competitors. You should spend a good amount of time watching what others are doing to understand the direction of the industry you are in.

CHAPTER 2:

IT ALL STARTS WITH A PLAN

Do you really need a Social Media Marketing Plan? The answer is simple, short, and direct: if you do not have a plan, you have little chance of success. Planning means making a strategy; without a strategy in the modern market, you do not sell. Planning means selling.

But is creating a true Social Marketing Plan easy or difficult? It depends, if for you it's the first time you can find some difficulties, but you will see in concrete that it's not very far from what you have already done in the past for your business—you have to reflect, compare, hypothesize, choose, understand, enhance, and finally to verify.

Using a metaphor, we could see Marketing as an orchestra and the Social Marketing Plan as the score to be followed. Every marketing action is the symphony played by a single musician; the score imposes rules, times, and style. The orchestra represents the set of many instruments that play, but they play alternately with a wise strategy. Every musical instrument is important, but necessary only if it follows the score. It is the conductor who decides what, when, and why.

Now, are you ready to make a Social Media Marketing Plan? Did you understand the need? To achieve a good plan you have to follow these six steps for they will simplify your life:

STEP 1: Identify the Correct Goals

The first step for any marketing strategy is to establish the goals you are hoping to achieve. A goal can be achieved the more you have a clear and more uncomplicated objective and if it can quickly adjust to changes in the market and business strategies. Without a concrete objective, there is no means to measure the progress of a marketing campaign. These social goals must, of course, be aligned with the broader marketing strategy.

One of the most used methods to identify the correct object to pursue is the SMART approach. SMART is an acronym used to remember the five characteristics of the correct objective: Specific (specific), Measurable (measurable), Attainable (attainable), Pertinent (relevant), Time-bound (with a fixed expiration).

An easy way to start your social media marketing plan is to give yourself at least two to three small goals. For example, you decide that you will share photos about the corporate culture on Instagram. You will do this by sending three photos a week with the goal of getting at least thirty shares a week and ten comments. Also, when posting your short articles on Facebook (at least twice a week), it would be better if it's related to content on your site or blog because you can directly link them and receive more visits. All activities must have a pre-established time and must be measurable and measured.

STEP 2: Market Analysis and Competition Analysis

The second step is to do a real market analysis of what can be done on every single social network and what your competitors are doing, apparently taking inspiration from international success stories, perhaps from your sector.

STEP 3: Voice and Style

Each company has its style and image that is usually reflected in every action: how the sales show up, the stand presented at the fair, the brochures, the business cards, the website, and so on. The company communicates through branding; it simply does so with its headquarters and warehouse, through furniture, colors, and its logo. The actions on social media must invariably express the style and the image that the company has strategically chosen to communicate. The Marketing Manager must be able to make social users perceive what the company wants them to see.

STEP 4: The Tools and the Channel

When you are well aware of the company style to communicate, all you need to do is identify the tools and channels you want to use. For example, LinkedIn and Facebook to create ad hoc posts on company products and services, Twitter to convey content with links to blog posts and website, Instagram to communicate photographs about corporate style, and Pinterest to communicate style and also to present Infographics on company services and the technologies identified.

Among the tools, we must include the Web Tools that were born in recent years, dedicated to the editorial management of content on social media. Well-known tools such as Hootsuite, TweetDeck, ManageFlitter, and many others, are essential for the management and analysis of social marketing.

STEP 5: Content Plan

The fifth step gives you the opportunity to reassemble all the previous steps in a single tool, creating a real content plan with precise timing divided by days, weeks, and months.

The editorial calendar must reflect the objectives identified, the chosen market strategy, the company style, and the pre-established tools or channels.

For example, if your purpose on Instagram is to generate contacts and on Facebook is to communicate the corporate image, you must make sure that your calendar represents well these two objectives (in terms of timing, type of message, the tool used, editorial consistency over time, and the number of weekly posts).

*in the photo above: an example of a simple calendar made in Microsoft Excel.

Step 6: Constant Check

Having implemented a Social Marketing Plan with its editorial strategy, it becomes crucial to be able to measure its progress and success, perhaps even the ROI (return on investment). Also for this step, as for the fourth, it is essential to use dedicated tools such as Google Analytics (analysis Blog, Website, Newsletter, Landing pages, etc.). For some time, Twitter has also been offering its Analytics for free. These and other tools allow you to analyze in detail a large amount of data grouped by type, bringing a clear picture of what works and what does not, which social media leads to more visits to the website, and which other social media website or social media scheme can turn the social media users into active contacts.

CHAPTER 3:

BEING CONSISTENT AND NINE OTHER IMPORTANT ASPECTS

Are you a small business and want to start a Social Media Marketing activity to promote your business? If the answer is yes, below you will find ten rules to follow for a successful SMM.

1. **Do not improvise.** Before opening your social media accounts and starting to publish, analyze the target audience and from its characteristics, realize a strategy that provides the guidelines to follow in all areas of communication, from the choice of channels to the definition of contents
2. **Give the public what they want.** Create quality content, provide information, give advice, and bring curiosity that can interest and engage your audience.
3. **Do not be too promotional.** Avoid talking only about your company or your products. The goal of social networks is to create conversations. Do not make classic advertising.
4. **Interacting with the audience.** Respond quickly to questions or comments from your audience. Through social media, you must create human and real relationships.
5. **Publish regularly.** Stick to an editorial calendar that provides for a periodic and constant publication based on your availability.

6. **Monitor the market.** Try to stay up-to-date with changes in your target market to change your strategy based on new trends or needs.
7. **Define evaluation metrics.** What do you want to achieve with your social activity? Do you want to increase your visibility? Do you want to increase the company sales? Or, do you want to get leads? Based on your goals, define the most appropriate metrics for evaluating the results.
8. **Monitor the results.** Analyze the behavior of your audience, interactions with your social accounts, and visits to the site. Once the metrics have been defined, constantly check that the results obtained are in line with those expected and, if not, make some strategic changes.
9. **Do not be in a hurry.** Social Media Marketing does not provide immediate results, but it is an activity that requires competence, patience, and, above all, constancy.
10. *"1 is greater than 0 or is it?"* Accounts not updated are a risk to the company's online reputation. So if you have little time available, avoid opening a thousand different social pages and then abandoning them. Alternatively, you can contact external consultants who, on the basis of your specific needs, will be able to optimize your Social Media Marketing activity.

CHAPTER 4:

THE BIG THREE – INSTAGRAM, FACEBOOK, AND YOUTUBE

A lot of people approaching social media marketing for the first time think that the key is to be on every social media website. The truth, however, is that it's much better to focus only on the platforms that people use the most. Right now, Instagram, Facebook, and YouTube are the most used social networks so we will focus on those three.

Instagram

Available at first for iOS devices only, the version for Android was born in 2012, allowing a faster deployment of the application and a significant increase in the number of subscribers to the platform. It is only as a result of this great growth that Mark Zuckerberg (founder of Facebook) understands its potential, so much so he decided to buy Instagram to turn it into a powerful social network, almost as long as the longest-running Facebook.

According to the Instagram blog, registered users in June 2018 were 1 billion, and data continues to grow. This makes us understand that Instagram is a social network not yet saturated and with much more to give to its users, so it proves a suitable platform for the development of new strategies of social media marketing—thanks to the use of visual storytelling with the aid of the many new features offered by the developers.

How to Succeed on Instagram

Instagram is a rather unusual social networking platform, unlike how other social networks such as Facebook or Twitter prevail. Thanks also to the lower average age of users, a more informal behavior characterized by immediacy and sharing of the moment.

In synergy with other social networks, Instagram is therefore increasingly used to highlight a less serious part of the brand linked to the story, people, life, or in other words, the "behind the scenes". Instagram is also being used to show a more creative side linked to the playful and artistic aspect.

Using a Business Account

Business profiles arrived in Italy in June 2016 and brought very useful news for all companies that use Instagram in their social media marketing strategy.

If you are a freelancer or a company, if you have not already done so, we recommend switching immediately. Simply enter the settings and tap on "Switch to Business Profile". At this point, you will not have to do anything but associate the linked Facebook page and indicate the contact options such as email and phone number.

By providing this data correctly, when users will land on your Business profile, they will be able to contact you directly without too many steps: just tap on "Call" or "Email". In addition, for the companies that have activated the Instagram Shopping function, the item "Products" will appear.

Once switched to Business Profile, a graphic icon will appear at the top right, namely "Insights".

The data shown are as follows:

- Impression and reach of your posts
- Photos with more interactions
- Insights data on Instagram Stories
- Data on followers
- Insights related to promotions

Instagram Biography: How to Write It

It is necessary to start from the details to implement a marketing strategy on Instagram, that is the care of the bio field.

It is important to know that within this section, it is mandatory to be as clear as possible, using the keywords that best identify the sector to which the company belongs. Recently, the platform introduced the possibility of inserting hashtags into the bio, making profiles easier to find.

The Instagram biography can contain a maximum of 150 characters and must be written with extreme care because, together with the profile image, this is what will prompt the user to click on the "Follow" button and to click on the "Call to Action".

Tone of Voice

First of all, it is necessary to define a tone of voice consistent with the values of the brand but which is in line with the target audience, that is the potential members of the community. To define the ToV, it is necessary to build a social media monitoring activity, that is the monitoring of user conversations.

This type of activity can be verified through suitable online tools such as Radian, Socialbakers, and many others.

Listening to conversations that revolve around certain keywords useful for your Instagram Marketing strategy will be of fundamental importance to understand how users express themselves and what problems and needs they would like to see resolved. All these are essential when studying a digital communication strategy.

Emojis

The use of emoji is by no means a child's practice; on the contrary, they can be used as a creative list for the division of application fields.

The visual content attracts much more than the text, consequently putting emoticons that help to outline the bio. It is a way to get the user's attention.

Another trick is to wrap between sentences to better clarify who you are, what you do, and to Call to Action to the user.

Call to Action (CTA)

In an Instagram Marketing strategy, it is always necessary to include a clear Call to Action to users. Lines such as "Visit our website" or "Follow us on Facebook and Twitter" are CTAs in all respect, and it is necessary that the message is clear to users and traceable to the company, using, for example, a tracking code of Google Analytics.

The Importance of Storytelling

Why has visual storytelling become fundamental in any digital strategy? It is clear: recent research has shown that users have an average attention threshold of 8 seconds. This shows the need for companies to be able to create attractive tools to ensure that the user's eye stops to read and watch content.

Storytelling means telling stories for persuasive communication, especially in politics, economics, and business. With the advent of social networks, users want to read and see original stories. This is why companies are required continuous innovation in the art of storytelling and emotion.

Self-referencing does not pay any more: it is necessary to use tools like Instagram to create narrative universes useful for community involvement.

To be able to create a good strategy for Instagram Marketing, it is of fundamental importance to experiment to find the correct and most appreciated way by the users. The feed created must be homogeneous so as not to confuse the community, which means that if you deal with catering, it makes no sense to publish travel content or other topics not closely related.

To have a good following on Instagram, you have to start from an excellent visual content: if the content is interesting and engaging, users will stop to read the caption. Within this field, it is necessary to tell stories involving the microblogging technique.

Instagram, like Facebook, offers fairly daily news, such as 60-second videos, Instagram Stories, photo albums, and IGTV. This is why it is always experimenting with new techniques for creating engagement within the community.

Speaking of 60-second videos, if you have included them in your strategy, we recommend using Instagram video apps like Boomerang, Diptic, or Flipagram.

Create a Content Marketing Strategy on Instagram

The first thing to do once we have identified our target audience is to structure the right content marketing strategy.

It is not enough to "be on Instagram" to be able to say you use this medium. Instead, it is necessary to study a creative path that allows the user who follows the brand to receive interesting contents, obviously respecting the Tone of Voice, the image, and positioning of the company; through this path, we can bring the user to become an ambassador and customer of the company.

To give a concrete (and simple) example: if the company is in the food sector, you will have to create a content marketing strategy that aims to give culinary directions such as recipes, ingredients, and raw materials. The contents should not be strictly related to the sale of the product but must serve to create an interaction and a relationship of trust with the user, who will then be interested in accessing the social network also because he or she finds interesting content on the company feed.

Create an Editorial Plan and an Editorial Calendar

Once a clear content marketing strategy has been identified and shared with all team members, we can proceed to summarize what has been decided so far within the editorial plan for the social network. It means creating a document with objectives, targets, and ways of creating content within a material that becomes the guide to consistently create future content to be posted on Instagram.

These contents will be programmed and inserted into an editorial calendar. Having an editorial calendar is essential because it allows you to never run out of content, as these are decided on time with certain deadlines and with equally certain managers.

An editorial calendar is therefore made up of specific posts, inserted into a weekly and monthly calendar to be followed to make sure you never run out of posts. Ideally, if we believe we have enough content, we could also post on Instagram every day, which means structuring an editorial calendar that is already covering several months. It is, however, desirable to have a calendar that requires posting two or three times a week.

Interact with Followers and Create a Community

Creating a community on Instagram is very important to create a Comment Marketing activity, a strategy based on comments on photos similar to those published by your company. The use of Instagram Bot is increasingly frequent, allowing follow-up and commenting based on who uses specific hashtags within the caption.

The problem of Comment Marketing with the Bots is that it does not lead to the real creation of the community, as a simple "Nice" or a little heart is not enough to interact with the relevant public. For this reason, for the creation of a community, it is always better to search through a hashtagged photos in line with your brand and to comment on them manually and regularly, writing something that also leads to an answer and intrigues the user so much to push them to follow you in turn.

How to Use Influencers

What are the influencers? Influencers are people with a significant following on Instagram, who may then have the power to direct users who follow them to a particular brand or company.

Influencers are usually rather sectorial and followed assiduously by those who are interested in a specific topic, so they can contact to look for a relationship with their brand if the target between their followers and those of the company is coherent. You can structure a co-marketing strategy with a shared hashtag or, in the case of companies in the fashion industry, for example, use them as brand ambassadors through their posts. In case of events (such as festivals, games, or other happenings), they can be invited to create awareness on the specific event.

Create Contest on Instagram

The creation of a contest on Instagram is a very widespread practice to stimulate engagement in the community already formed, for the improvement of brand awareness and the generation of new qualified leads.

Stimulating Competition

For participation in an Instagram contest, users must feel encouraged to share personal photographs with a decidedly vast network. To convince and involve the community, it is necessary to have a stimulating idea that will somehow leverage the emotional sphere of the individual.

An example of an emotional contest can be that of Vetoquinol, where users have been asked to take up moments of play and fun with their four-legged friend.

Interesting Prizes

When users decide to participate in an online competition, it is very easy for them to try to win the prize at stake. The higher the perceived value (economic and effective), the higher the chances of participation by users.

If the company deals with sales of technological products, the raffling of the latest tablet model released on the market will be more incentive than the awarding of simple custom covers.

Furthermore, the prizes of competition must always be in line with the promoter's core business to avoid confusing users about your field of activity.

Studying a Promotion Strategy

In addition to the classic promotional strategies, such as ADV, newsletters, postings on the page, and shares, you can use the hashtags on Instagram. Each competition must have its own hashtag designed for the occasion, which allows to group in a simple way all the contents published by the users.

Instagram Stories: How to Exploit Them

The Instagram Stories were introduced in the second half of 2016, after witnessing the Snapchat boom especially in the very young audience (target between 15 and 25 years).

The Stories have potentials thanks to their usability: they serve to offer special contents that disappear after 24 hours. Applied to Instagram Marketing can be very useful, as you can create exclusive content for creating engagement within particular communities.

For example, you can use them to show moments of exclusive events to engage the fanbase or to offer special discounts and promotions lasting only 24 hours. Or, again, if you have a verified Instagram profile, you will have the opportunity to show the products offered by the online shop by entering the direct link. This way you will not require too many steps to users, who will feel more incentive to proceed with the purchase.

This technique is often used by blogger and entrepreneur Chiara Ferragni, who in her stories mixes moments of everyday life with decidedly more commercial content in which she shows the products she designed and created, referring directly to her e-shop.

Features like questions, surveys, and emoji appreciation have made them even more interactive, contributing to the enormous success that Instagram Stories are having between users and companies.

How to Measure the Results

Creating a strategy for the Instagram profile is useful. Periodically check if the objectives, whether medium-term or long-term, have been recognized. Set specific goals on how to engage more users and how to generate more followers. You will then check, in addition to the mere and simple "engagement" on the platform, if those followers have also become customers or users of the product or service.

To measure the results, you should correctly set the conversion funnel and be able to obtain quantifiable data from the analytics platforms set. If the goal is to make sure that users register for a service on your site, it will be important to identify how many users have come through the Instagram channel

Facebook

In 2018, Facebook remains one of the main channels for marketing but, like everything in the digital world, it changes regularly and every so often. At the beginning of this year, Facebook changed the algorithm of its Newsfeed. They decided to prioritize the posts of relatives and friends (the system considers the profiles with which a user contacts more often), to those that cause discussions and conversations, and to the publication of the pages that a user has chosen to see first (See First in the preferences of the News Feed). Under these conditions, marketing on Facebook becomes a challenge.

The best content on Facebook is the one that involves and stimulates communication. There is no single formula to write a successful content, but there are some tricks that can help you increase the effectiveness of your posts:

- Publish posts in the best time. Analyze when your audience is online to optimize your publication time.

- Evaluate your audience. Track the performance of your posts and find out what they like most to your target and what is the winning content for your editorial plan. I will talk shortly about the importance of analytics.
- Take advantage of current issues and trends. Find out what are the topics that infect users using services like Google Trends, Trending Topic on social media, or follow the calendar of events for your industry (even local ones, if they are relevant to you).
- Use the questions as Call to Action to encourage users to leave comments under your publication.
- Miscellaneous content. The predictability of your posts can damage your strategy. Try different types of content and alternating topics and formats of your posts or publications so your audience won't get bored.

The video format is interesting not only because Facebook tends to prioritize it, but also because, among the various types of content that you can publish on your page, it is the one most loved by users.

Here is a small selection of tips for video optimization for Facebook:

- Upload videos directly to Facebook because posts with YouTube links lose visibility (Facebook gives priority to videos uploaded on its platform)
- Ideal format: Facebook recommends using MP4 and MOV. A complete list of recommended formats you can find Facebook recommends uploading videos with a maximum duration of 15 seconds, with attractive and high-quality content.
- The public on Facebook also appreciates long-read texts when they are well-written; if the theme is current, it is

easy to generate conversions. Why shouldn't the same rule work for the video?

- Upload the videos with subtitles (about 85 % of videos is shown without the sound) and do not forget to add a title and a small description to make people understand the subject of the video right away.
- Video streaming is another type of content that Facebook likes so much and can get yourself a good organic reach. When you create a Live on Facebook, all your friends and followers will be notified of the start of a new stream, so everyone can follow and comment on your video live.

Content marketing and content curation are two of the words that most marketers will be interested in this year. Content marketing is a much more extensive approach that is not limited to the Facebook channel but can play a decisive role on the same platform. I speak of the choice and creation of content to be conveyed in their fan page that, if chosen accurately, with an attractive graphics and communicated in the right way (sometimes even in the right time), it can become "viral", reaching even outside of our primary user target. However, by doing so, it could give us the advantage of expanding our brand positioning to other target users, who until then thought we were not interested in us. Translated into simple words: the content conveyed on the page, through sharing and "like", can attract new users to know our brand and start to follow it from the page.

Facebook Insights provide much more data than before, and the service is almost similar to Google Analytics. Periodically going to "combing" the data helps to understand better what are the most appreciated contents by users and those that generate greater shares (now, we can also know what are the comments with negative "sentiment" even if the service is not very reliable).

From the analysis of our pages and those of our customers, it appears that quality images (especially those released for the first time and then created in-house) and videos (in second place) are those that reach the best level of engagement (likes, shares, comments) and consequently are more likely to spread our brand/product and making it known to new users.

YouTube

YouTube is a web-based video sharing platform that was set up 11 years ago by the trio Chad Hurley, Jawed Karim, and Steve Chen. The idea of creating a social video sharing platform was particularly risky but diabolically apt.

A website at the time was merely an idea, but in a few years, it has become the reference point for millions of Internet users who upload movies of any kind every day, while millions of users spend their time watching these videos every single day.

The growth of YouTube has become exponential when the giant of Mountain View, Google, has decided to acquire the company and liquidate the three founders handsomely.

The commercial operation turned out to be a winner, Google, in fact, has made YouTube the third most visited website in the world, being only behind the same search engine of Google to the social network par excellence Facebook.

Since YouTube has come to life and has become what it is today, we have studied the phenomenon, and our goal is to promote and give visibility to our customers also through this colossus of social media.

To date, YouTube is a hotbed of new talent, music, entertainment, and entertainment in general. It is also an immense advertising window for companies and individuals who have chosen the

Internet as a vehicle to promote their product and their professionalism.

The promotion through YouTube is one of the biggest opportunities that this social platform makes available and through the right skills, we will know how to enhance and take the best of what YouTube offers us.

Success comes through YouTube views, visits obtained by watching that specific video or that particular channel.

In this case, every user registered on the platform (after the marriage with Google, just a Big G account) can become a publisher, an author, a director, and a screenwriter of their YouTube channel at one fell swoop, which will be instantly reachable throughout the world; you will be the official disseminator of your ideas. Or, you can simply be a spectator with decidedly active connotations together with many other viewers, which could determine the success of a video or the same YouTube channel and also a reflection of a brand or an idea.

The YouTube Views are therefore the number of views that the video gets, not to be confused with the YouTube Likes, which instead indicate your liking related to the video or channel viewed.

The second concept is not entirely different from what made Facebook famous and is one of the first parameters to keep in mind to achieve success.

Making a video and uploading it to YouTube is easy, but it is even easier to end up in obscurity and never reach the desired visibility. Our goal is to provide the right information not to end up in a dead end and not remain anonymous.

Whether you are a company or a private individual with a new idea, you can come up with a promotion for your YouTube Marketing; you can think of a solid marketing plan.

As with any product or service, even YouTube has its own good rules and its proper techniques to stay on the crest of the wave in which should be studied and applied daily.

YouTube Search Engine Optimization (YouTube SEO) has some basic steps to follow, not to be one of the many on the video sharing platform, but to be among the protagonists offering greater visibility on search engines.

Among the measures made available, we mentioned some that may seem trivial, but they are all essential to get to the top and stay there.

The metadata is undoubtedly fundamental as it is the series of everything we do in the digital world. It is all the additional information we can input as a part of our video. Descriptions in the YouTube video and channel are an example. If there are subtitles, they are also used as an indexing parameter for a video (the same speech is intended to be extended in the same way between channel and video).

Accurate description in the process of creating the channel and uploading the video, in short, should not be taken lightly, but instead must be carefully studied and weighted.

Here are some interesting tips that will help you in your journey on YouTube.

As for blogs, you can try to attract public attention by proposing content that interests visitors. You can simply view the public Google and YouTube statistics on the Internet to know the contents that best interest the visitors or audience. In this regard, I suggest you turn to Google Trends, the free tool made available by big G where users can find out what are the most viewed videos on YouTube and the most searched terms on Google.

To use it, connect to the main web page of Google Trends. You will be shown all the videos on YouTube that have been more successful on the net during the last hours. You can refine your search further by using the special menu at the top. I suggest you take a look at the trends on Google. Click on the button with the three horizontal lines that can be found at the top left, then click on the item attached to the menu that is shown. Click on USA from the drop-down menu to select the country located at the top right and choose an eventual reference category from the one located on the left. Then, consult the results below.

You can get an even more precise idea of the research trends by clicking on the button with the three horizontal lines located at the top left, choosing the item Trends in searches from the menu displayed, selecting Italy from the drop-down menu at the top, and consulting the various results.

Another great tool to get an idea of the trends on YouTube is VidStatX. It is a service that lets you know the most successful YouTube videos and channels in the last period.

Create Interesting Videos

Once you have identified the right topics, you can upload themed videos using catchy titles and optimized tags corresponding to the most searched keywords by people on the Internet.

For example, if you own a software company and you find that a lot of people search in Google on how to speed up Windows 10, make a video explaining how to improve the performance of the latest Microsoft Home Operating System (HomeOS). Set a captivating phrase for the video title, such as "How to Speed Up Windows 10 free, tested, and running at 100%". Tag some terms such as "speed up Windows 10", "optimize Windows 10", "speed up PC", and so on.

By doing so, you will have a good chance that by searching on Google or YouTube, many people will find your video and decide to subscribe to the channel.

Advertise the Channel

When you create your videos, do not forget to add in the video itself and in its description some references to the previously uploaded videos on your channel (possibly related to the topic covered in the current video) and invite viewers to subscribe to the channel (without being too insistent, of course).

To entice visitors to view your other videos relevant to the current one and to subscribe to your YouTube channel, you can use the comment feature in videos. This is a feature made available by YouTube to insert "comics" in crucial points of the videos in which you invite users to subscribe to the channel or refer them to other videos that may be of interest to them using direct links.

If you think you have made some very interesting videos, like a guide or a review that can help people solve problems or avoid wrong purchases, you could try to advertise yourself by pointing out the video to famous blogs and sites that deal with the topic you have spoken in the video. A fruitful collaboration could also be born!

If you own a blog or a website, you could try to post your videos on it as well as advertise your YouTube channel with special buttons. How do you do it? Simple: all you need to do is connect to this YouTube page and find the button you prefer most among those available. Then, download it to your computer and insert the downloaded image on the main page of your site or blog (maybe in the sidebar). Add to it a link to tie-up to your YouTube channel or a specific video, depending on your needs. By doing these operations, you should be able to earn some visits from casual users.

Also, if you have a video on your channel that you want to promote more than any other, put it in the foreground. To do so, access the main page of your YouTube channel by clicking on the button with the three horizontal lines located at the top left and selecting the item My Channel from the menu that is shown to you. Then, click on the button to add a featured video. Next, choose the video you want to feature in the channel, click the Apply button, and you're done.

Some Recommendations

Finally, I want to recommend some basic rules to increase your views on YouTube. Never fall into those systems that try to steal money promising you stratospheric increases in visits because, in most cases, they are scams (or illicit techniques to inflate visits) and never abuse keywords in the tags and titles of your videos.

Use optimized titles and tags, as I have explained before, but make sure that they are relevant to the video content. Do not use keywords related to news events or celebrities when they have nothing to do with the video you are uploading; you could increase your channel visits in a few days, but you would lose any credibility and long play. You risk finding yourself with zero visits also loading contents interesting.

Moreover, as I have told you at the beginning of the guide, considering to increase the views on YouTube is essential to work, giving space to constancy and perseverance, and trying to produce something that has a real value for the beholder. To understand better how to proceed, I suggest you follow what are the most famous YouTube channels and will soon see the difference in your numbers.

CONCLUSION

Thank you for making it through to the end of *Social Media Marketing: How to use Social Media Marketing to Convert People into Customers*! Let's hope it was informative and able to provide you with all the tools you need to achieve your goals whatever they may be. Just because you've finished this book doesn't mean there is nothing left to learn on the topic—expanding your horizons is the only way to find the mastery you seek.

After reading all the tips and procedures from this guidebook, the next step to start doing whatever it is that you need to do to ensure that you are now able to develop amazing content. You need to do some researching on what to include on your contents, making sure that they are true and accurate. Being always in the know helps to increase your customers, users, and audience. If you find that you still need help in getting you started, you will likely have better results by creating a schedule that you hope to follow—including strict deadlines for various parts of the tasks as well as the overall completion of your preparations.

Studies show that complex tasks that are broken down into individual pieces, including individual deadlines, have a much higher chance of being completed when compared to something that has a general need of being completed but no real timetable for doing so. Even if it seems silly, go ahead and set your deadlines for completion—complete with indicators of success and failure. After you have successfully completed all your required preparations, you will be glad you did. For example, you can think about practicing one new social media marketing trick every day before becoming a general master of the power of your words. It is your choice, and it is the beauty of mastering your writing ability.

Once you have tried the same strategies many times, you are going to see amazing results.

Finally, if you find this book useful in any way, a review on Amazon is always appreciated!

www.ingramcontent.com/pod-product-compliance
Lightning Source LLC
Chambersburg PA
CBHW031507210526
45463CB00003B/1112